New Orleans BORN

A Poetic Odyssey

PHYLLIS B. PARUN

Copyright © 2019 PHYLLIS B. PARUN

All Rights Reserved. No part of this publication may be reproduced or transmitted in any means, electronic or mechanical, including photocopying, recording, or any information storage and retrieval system, without permission in writing. For permissions contact the publisher or author.

Cover art and all illustrations are solely owned by the author and requires permissions.

Permission to make copies of any part of this work can be submitted in email to pbpstudio@yahoo.com

Cover Design and Illustrations by Phyllis Parun

ISBN: 978-1-7323560-0-9

BERNARD PRESS
Publisher

New Orleans, Louisiana

Inaugural Edition

In loving memory of each member
of my wonderful, gifted family
who in a spirit of community,
brought family, friends and neighbors together,
generously sharing their enthusiasm
and enormous talents;
without their guidance and inspiration
there would have been no art,
no music, no poetry, no writing.

And to all the neighbors and friends who
joining together brought joy into all our lives,
thusly, making life a beautiful art
to be savored forever.

Phyllis B. Parun

Part One (3-34)

"Pity me not for the beauties passed away."
Edna St. Vincent Millay

*

Life Leaves *3*
New Orleans My home *4*
Childhood *6*
Flames Flicker *9*
Early Memories *11*
Gone *13*
My Brother Myself *14*
Late Summer *17*
My Father, My Coach *19*
Mementoes *20*
Grandmother's House *22*
The Singer *25*
Retired *26*
Rooting Around *28*
Mother Music 31
Map *33*
Tea Brews *34*

Life leaves
Swiftly,
   Like a flock of geese.

"Lafitte's Blacksmith Shop," New Orleans, charcoal, Phyllis Parun, 1956.

NEW ORLEANS, MY HOME

New Orleans, my home
   place of birth
   of family tombs
   failed dreams
   dashed fame
and lost love.

Who are you
    persisting in my consciousness
    with your familiar streets
    and European buildings
    entombing memories on every corner,
    hanging from architecture
    like so much Spanish moss on 300 year old Oaks.

Who are you
    to occupy my only time on this planet
    my brain dying a little more each day
    from the summer heat   and
    this vacuous coffeehouse society, few artists
    talking aesthetics in the streets, while I
    longing for some meaningful depth
    find no philosopher's renaissance here.

It's no Paris in the 20's!

"The Family Room," 407 East Morris Ave., Hammond, La., 1947.

CHILDHOOD

Telephone
We had one   and it rang
in the unheated front of our cottage
near the front door
down the long narrow hallway
past the hall tree
past grandfather's rolltop desk -
Aunt Marie would pick up
the black bell-shaped receiver
switchboard operator
connecting her to the caller
She answering.

Radio
We had one   and listened
to favorite mystery stories
and classical music
after dinner
in the family room
off our kitchen
with the wood burning stove -
Sprawled out on the antique rug
with our coloring books and tinker toys,
mother and aunts in rocking chairs
crocheting and singing.

Automobile
We had one   and it was very reliable
my brother and I
swallowed up in the huge back seat
of that old Hudson
watched the asphalt street roll past
through a hole in the floor board
Radio playing on.

Years later   and
We had them
radios blaring from our bedrooms
dancing to Little Richard and Jerry Lee Lewis
Fats walkin' to New Orleans and
Elvis wearing blue suede shoes -
James Dean, Audrey Hepburn, Esther Williams
– our heroes.

Childhood!   Yes.
We had one.

Flames flicker on candles
Rain falls on roof tops
    Come, let us dance.

"Backyard Dollhouse," Hammond, La., **1947**.

EARLY MEMORIES

Early memories? I have none
None of my own, that is -
family creating mine   surely
but none mine
I adopted theirs -
They were my memory keepers
reporting what   I now remember so well
Childhood memories from cherished family photos,
experiences they relayed
while flipping through the family albums -
Those are my memories now
But as for mine   none.

Oh, wait! Yes,
there are some
as far back as 5 or maybe 7, who knows,
as I don't remember the
age of those memories
(Can memory have an age, I wonder?)

Yes!
I remember my brother and me playing croquet
and card games with our mother and aunts -
I might have been 9.

I remember
traveling in the Chevy Coupe
looking out of the back window
counting cars and competing
to see who guessed the model first.

Yes!
I remember
the sound of rubber tires on gravel road
Mother singing in the front seat
us singing along
Daddy doing the driving.
But, earlier than five, nothing -
No memories, except   what photos hold and
what family reported.

They were
my memory keepers.

Now
I keep
memories   for them.

Yes!
I remember.

GONE

   gone are
              the days

when the sun blazed yellow

                     all over the page

   and the smell of crayolas

                completely filled my room

"Sister, Brother," Hammond La., studio photographer, 1945.

MY BROTHER, MYSELF

Deep into the land of grieving I went
Traces of our childhood
still embraced by my heart.

Born of the same parents,
Soul and roots
Melded by blood,
Solidified by traditions,
Jointed by childhood,
Loyal and faithful -
No questions asked;
We, brother and sister.

My brother Myself

You, more like mother
Me, more like father
We, family   always.

Were it not for them,
I would never have been your sister
Nor you my brother.

Were it not for them,
I would never have known you
Nor you me.

Same cloth different patterns,
You, the player of board games,
Me, the creative artist,
You, the American eater,
Me, the macrobiotic,
You, a religious Christian,
Me, a spiritual explorer.
So different, yet so much the same.

My brother Myself

Playmates, teammates, life explorers -
We had family inspiration
And momentum,
We had each other
Holding together through six decades,
Burying each family member -
Familial love carrying us through.

My brother Myself

With more years behind me than in front,
Now compressed into these memories,
Times which kindly cradled me then
Cradle me now.

My brother Myself.

Late summer
A golden mist of sunrise falls.
It's afternoon.

"My Father, gentleman sportsman," photograph, Phyllis Parun, 2017.

MY FATHER, MY COACH

In your absence
I, lost in this vastness of this world
Trying to be the all-around athlete you were -
Ask your indulgence
For not carrying on as you would.
I entreat you now,
Be my inspiration in this wasteland –
As you once were
When I was a child
With you by my side
Urging me to achieve
my personal best.

"Archives," photograph, Phyllis Parun, 2017.

MEMENTOES

Grandfather's antique chair
Grandmother's embroidered pillow
The cane rockers   one for each family member
Aunt Mary's crystal rosary
Godmother's thimble and button collection.
The turn-of-the-century upright piano.

Mother's delicate pencil drawings
saved by her sisters then passed to me,
Father's books of inspirational poetry
he kept close during the war,
Brother's Boy Scout knife
and his first speed chess clock.
Years of joy and years of sorrow!

And when I die, and these things pass on,
Will they become   to their new owners
mere droppings from someone else's family table
assessed solely for their antique value?
Who will cherish them   as I do now?

Tears of sorrow, tears of joy
This   living   with
family memorabilia.

"Grandmother Mare Parun and Family,"
photograph, Phyllis Parun, 2017.

GRANDMOTHER'S HOUSE

This ancestral home
the scent of three generations
linger   still

Aunt Mary, there
in her patio garden   cultivating poinsettias
Uncle Peter   at his oak desk
studying accounting
Grandmother   at the cooking pot
making oyster stew.
It smells like home

And now
my brother's photograph
still on the round oak family table
where he once ate now an altar
his ashes in the parlor
where his bed once stood

This dying place
grandfather, grandmother, aunt,
and brother   all -
passed on   here.

Memories live here now

When sold
the nouveaux riche
would gut these plaster walls to the studs -
modern conquistadors,
stripping decades of immigrant life
substituting sheetrock, pop culture, and gentrification
all doomed to the short life
and the death due them -
as so much trash from post-industrial civilization.
- mere parody of its former self!

Grandmother's house,
ancestral home
place of love and wisdom
now a relic of cultural memory
slated for erasure
in this era of deletions.

- I lament

"Christabel," charcoal drawing, Phyllis Parun, 1959.

THE SINGER

She was born with that voice
absolute pitch, musical skill extraordinaire,
never a faulty delivery did pass her lips
too many words made her sick
music   was her forte;
when she sang scales
only a nightingale could compete
with the beauty of her sound.
She was My Fair Lady,
Lilly Pons, and Maria Callas
and when she left
she took the music with her.

*"**The Fibonacci Staircase**,"* (Arne Jacobsen, Royal Hotel, Copenhagen), photograph, Phyllis Parun, 2003.

RETIRED

I am retired now.
Mother died   father too,
Aunts, godmother and uncle   followed.
And then
My only brother.

I am retired now
No longer a daughter,
No longer a niece,
Not a godchild,
And now
No sister to anyone.

I am retired   now.

I did not leave my home,
My home left me   here
in this alien land

And I, feeling like an abandoned child
With what remains of family inspiration and love
Reside within me   now
While I, longing for who I am no longer,
seek who I was before.
deep into the long-ago childhood I go
looking for what was there

for me -

Now.

"Self-Portrait," New Orleans, Phyllis Parun, 2017.

ROOTING AROUND

Rooting around the museum of my memories
I find the many lives I have lived   in this finite one.
I find those of my own choosing
Alongside the precious hand-me-down lives
of family members   no longer with me.

I find the sheet music we sang at the family piano,
The games we played on card tables, courts and lawns
I find the tools of all their many arts and trades
And I - wanting to be each one of them -
studied their every move
listened attentively to every lesson taught
imitated every gesture each made.
Thusly, I lived all the lives they lived before me.
(And lived them well, I did!)

Among these ruins is an abandoned civilization,
While I   I am the shrine
and the keeper of its memories.

"My Mother, My Teacher," photograph, Phyllis Parun, 2017.

MOTHER MUSIC

I heard Mother's voice   call
from the other side
of this thin line between us

Me, dressed in flesh
She, in spirit.

Her lips move,
I hear her read
the favorite poem
she once read
to this   child

that I am

Still.

\

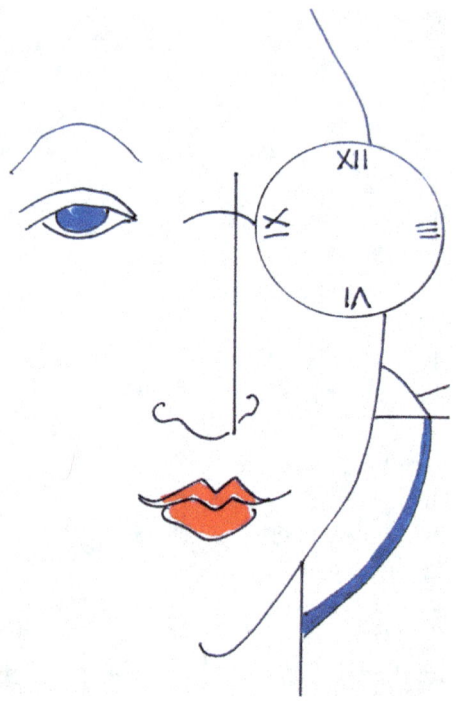

"Time-Released Self," ink drawing,
Phyllis Parun, 1983.

MAP

They dropped me off here!
I travel this road   now
Without them.

I live in this place   now
Without them.

Following the one map they left me -

This me

   that   I am.

Tea brews
Rain songs fall on gutters.
    I am home.

Part Two (37-44)

"A life should leave deep tracks." *Ruth Ryan*

*

Sunrise *37*
Pilgrimage to Paris *39*
The Line *40*
That's a Nice Tomb *42*
The Dancer *45*
Immortality *46*
Sunday *48*
Worship *49*
Where Do I Live? *51*
Aprés Déluge *53*
Empty *54*
Sunrise in Bywater *55*
Nothing *57*
Goddess *59*
Today *60*
Ancient Oak *62*

Ah, sunrise falls,
on the summer afternoon -
      A golden mist.

"Street in Paris," photograph, Phyllis Parun, 2001.

PILGRIMAGE TO PARIS
and The Père Lachaise Cemetery

Paths and paths and paths
   of graves
   housing artists and writers
Now dead.

Paths and paths
   leading to more paths
   to eternal houses of
   once vibrant artists.
It's the year 2000
   and all these artists   now icy cold
lay in this damp, stony place.

Paris now a City of Phantoms
   and still the tourists come
   like so many hungry refugees
   from contemporary civilization
   seeking guidance from these graves
   and inspiration from the streets of Paris
   where these artists once walked
And from the stones they once walked upon.

"Line," ink on paper, Phyllis Parun, 2016.

THE LINE

It was to be just one line
one simple line   on paper
for an exhibition   that was all
her entire life in a line   one single line
a line with a past   her past
one line with dreams   her dreams
not those of ancestors nor parents nor teachers
only her singular dream   in one line -
visions emerging from her origins.

For days lines came and lines went
her efforts to duplicate   to repeat
to improve the line   failed
and failed   and failed.

With each brush stroke
there was only a new line
no corrections   no improvements
nothing new.

There was just one line   there
one simple line
some she enjoyed
some she did not,
some pleased her
some did not
some went into the trash
some did not.

Then one day   effortlessly
one flawless line graced the paper
one elegant simple line
with its own lyric   her lyric
one perfect meandering line -
her line.

"St. Louis Cemetery #3," New Orleans, photograph,
Phyllis Parun, 1998.

THAT'S A NICE TOMB

That's a nice tomb!
New Orleans is full of tombs
whole cities for the dead
above ground tombs big as houses
embellished with finely carved
figurative sculpture.

Here the Dead are dead
the living are dead -
walking dead
Everyone here is dead.

Bodies haunting the streets
taking up space
roaming around
looking for meaning
looking for love
looking for sex and drugs
Finding only the walking dead.

Tombs
City of tombs
City of living dead
walking dead
buried dead
reincarnated dead
and I, foolishly looking for a solution
to my heartbreaking sorrow
among these ruins.

"*Dancer*," ink on paper, Phyllis Parun, 1983.

THE DANCER

She danced   through childhood
ballet, tap, waltz
as a teen it was jitterbug, foxtrot, mambo
still later there was tai chi and qigong.
Always she danced
she never stopped dancing.
Her body was lean, yoga lean, qigong lean, dancer lean
and when she walked   it was a dancer's walk
toes pointed when she walked
arms moving like the wings of a swan.

Painting and poetry came just as naturally;
when she painted her brush danced
when she wrote her phrases danced.

When she was happy or blue
or needed something fresh
she daydreamed of old New Orleans
of dancing house parties
of high school hops.
She brought back her verve
by dancing in her studio
to Blue Monday, Good Golly Miss Molly
and Sweet Little Sixteen   until exhausted.
And when she died   her spirit rose
into an azure sky
and danced among the clouds.

"Passage," Copenhagen photograph, Phyllis Parun, 2002.

IMMORTALITY

Before birth
Oblivion,
After death
Oblivion.

When you leave you will leave
the people you have loved,
the things you have cherished,
the work you have enjoyed -
all your precious memories
Even your footprints on the sands of time
will wash away in the tide
when you leave your ashes
in this finite realm
between birth and death.

Before birth
Oblivion
After death
Oblivion

If life has no meaning,
what value then

This magnificent beauty?

A poem
Lays on the altar, waiting,
Waiting for me.
> *It's Sunday.*

WORSHIP

This is my church
This poem.
It is she where I worship
And she who worships me.
There is none other.

It is the solemn word
The poignant phrase
The unseen, unspoken beauty
that I worship.
The poem, my altar
The prayer to life, my deity.

That is my church
Where I worship -
None other.

"The Self," clay, Phyllis Parun, 1960.

WHERE DO I LIVE?

Where do I live?
Certainly not here   in this banal modernity -
Perhaps in yet another century
in ancient or future worlds
Where tranquility and harmony abide
Where war and anger slumber.
Perhaps, I live beyond time
in ideals, in hopes and dreams
While you seem to live
in another place   another time -
While we, realms apart
separated   by many, many worlds
try to be here now   together
in this one
brief
moment
in time.

"Stravinsky's The Flood,"
glass window design, Phyllis Parun, 1977.

APRÈS DÉLUGE

So often I long for home -
for the old New Orleans   my New Orleans,
that New Orleans   I was born into, grew up in,
the New Orleans of my heart
now in my memories

And even though it is all   still here
the past and the present
the living and the dead
the fantasy and the reality
side by side.
Still I long for home
as if it wasn't.

Empty mind
Empty journal
   Full life.

SUNRISE IN BYWATER

In the quietude of the early morning
I am alone   in my antique house,
not another person to shatter
the beauties of my solitude
save my cat, demanding food.

As the sun rises over
this Creole neighborhood
with its quiet streets
singing birds and
falling leaves.
I sip tea
in the backyard garden
and greet the dawn.

"*Moonscape ,*" ink on paper, Phyllis Parun, 1996.

DOING NOTHING

Surrounded by
the hot Sun
the cool Moon
and tall Mountains,
you taught us
everything we needed to know
about Nothing
And I found it to be
more than enough.

(For Taoist teacher, Ken Cohen, 1998)

"Pilgrimage," ink on paper, Phyllis Parun, 2002.

I went to the Mountains
To meet a messenger of the Goddess -
And no one came to greet me.

(For Dr. Peter Kingsley, Esalen, 2004)

"Water," cut gouache on paper, Phyllis Parun, 2012.

TODAY AFTER THE FLOOD

Today I went to meet the Sun
   as she rose over Monterey Bay –
   her long, steady, golden rays brought warmth
   to these tired, damp bones.
Today I saw our mother, the water.
Today she was active,
   her white waves
   rolling into rocks.
Today she was not menacing.

Today her waves splashing over rocks,
   so strong a weak swimmer would be overcome,
   so strong a floating otter would sink,
   strong enough a sunbathing seal
   would be carried away.
Yet today she was not menacing,
   but contained in Monterrey Bay
   surrounded by a rock levy,
Today her splashing and rolling waters
   could not touch me,
   could not sink me,
   could not carry me away.
Today she does not threaten
   my very existence.
Today she gives me peace and solitude
And yet, she has the power to take it away.

Today I could enjoy her beauty,
   I could hear her roaring sounds,
I could accept her gift of life,
   knowing that
   just for today
to be alive is enough.

(After the flood of Karina, 2005)

"Ancient Oak," ink on paper, Phyllis Parun, 2002.

ANCIENT OAK

I see your stately, raw limbs have healed,
   sealed up over time -
Your slaughterer's orange spray paint still visible
   on the outer bark of some.
You still seem weary from the ordeal.

Old and sedentary
   you could not run
   from the barbarians and their saws.

Once your majestic limbs crawled along the earth
   providing natural play stations for joyful children
   now sadly replaced by a lifeless plastic version
   just steps away from you.
While you,
   still full of life and ancient wisdom
   rest in its shadows,
   forgotten by your children admirers
   your duck friends once embracing you
   with their daily presence
   are now missing too.
It's dusk
   and no one comes to feed them since the flood.

Some of your aged limbs   now cut off
   some still remaining, eaten away by water rot
   while those limbs sliced away in their prime of life
   are now gone from you forever.
While your roots
   resembling snakes
   spreading out from your aging trunk
   and gripping the earth
   still serve you well.

Part Three *(67-99)*

"Beauty is the language of care." *Alice Waters*

*

Poetry Awaits *67*
Beauty Salon *68*
The Model and Her Muse *71*
Full of Youth *72*
Age Approaches *73*
Poet's Life *75*
Poet's Cat *76*
Doors *78*
Early Morning *79*
Ghosts *81*
Poet's House *83*
No Down Spouts *84*
Lions *85*
Misfit *87*
Bittersweet *88*
Words *89*
Bio *90*
Beautiful Moment 91
Acknowledgements 93
Notes 95
Biography 98

Poetry awaits
The quietude of dawn.
        Sun rises.

BEAUTY SALON

I went for a hair cut.
Sitting in the salon chair
in front of a large mirror
the cutter ran her fingers through my hair.
Noticing the beginnings of grey
the salt among the pepper,
She remarked, "We could make you look younger –
get rid of some of those unwanted years."
Her words set me wondering,
Which years would those unwanted years be?
Would they be the ones in utero
when I was floating in the abyss of time?
Or were they those early years when father was
drafted and sent to Japan when I was a child at
play, drawing, dancing and singing?
Or did she mean my teenage years when mother
was sick with cancer and died?
I thought, those couldn't be the years she meant
as they were years of delight and love.
Perhaps, she meant my 20's, the academic college
years when I studied world philosophy and history?

Oh, no - not be those years. Those were years
of learning, adventure and making lifelong friends.
Instead she must have meant
  my developing 30's,
  my relationship exploring 30's,
  fine-and-decorative-arts-studio career 30's?
No, I don't think those are what she meant either.
Those years offered too many growthful challenges
  to be unwanted.
So maybe, it was the macrobiotic cooking 40's
 or the qigong teaching 50's?
Still these didn't seem the likely years
 to which she referred either
 as they were maturing years
 deepening my sense of who I was.

Which years did she think were "unwanted" then,
  unwanted as if they were
  an unwanted-unplanned-not-cared-for-child?
Which unwanted, unloved years did she mean?

Finally, unable to determine what she meant,
I just shrugged and replied,
"None of my years were unwanted,
and all of my grey is wanted
so I shall just keep it all just the way it is.
Thank you."

"Artist's Model," ink on paper, Phyllis Parun, 1994.

THE MODEL AND HER MUSE

She looked at me -
I was drawing
   focusing somewhere passed her
   passed the form that she was
   into another world
   a mere shadow of this one.
She looked at me,
   dead at me.
She didn't look passed me.
She looked directly into my eyes.
She looked at the person that I was
   sitting there in front of her.
She shattered my trance,
   the severed pieces
   fell down around me
   and I stood there naked   before her.

She was the model.
I was her muse.

FULL OF YOUTH

Still Full of youth
I get drunk on food
Stay up all night
Drinking tea and
Writing poetry
Past the sun's rising
And the songs of birds.

AGE APPROACHES

You don't see her coming
then she stands boldly in front of you
and sticks her tongue out at you.
You turn away from her
so she sits right down in front of you
and hums a familiar tune.
You ignore her once again.
then she moves right in ,
makes herself at home and
you're stuck with her —
Forever!

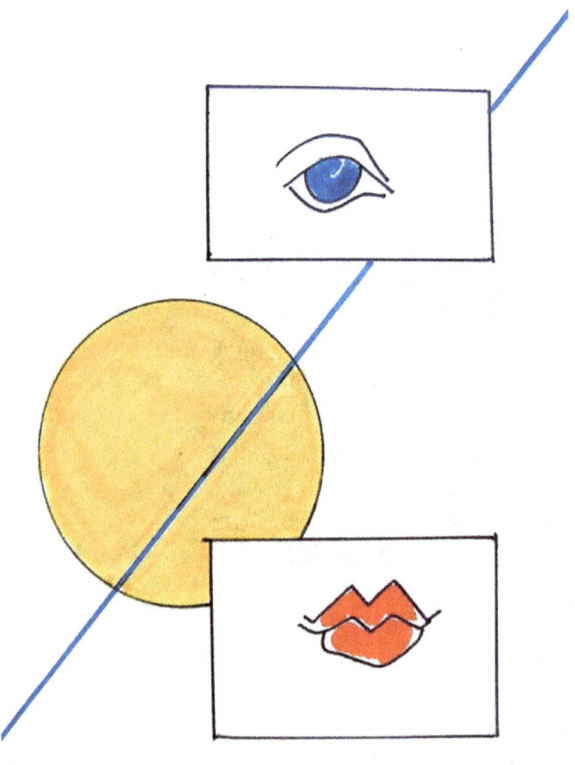

"Poet's Hours," ink drawing Phyllis Parun, 1983.

THE POET'S LIFE

I keep poets hours
Writing 'til dawn
Sleeping 'til noon
Following my muse
  everywhere she goes
  with the tip of my pen.
Turning the ringer off the phone
Basking in the solitude of my home
  curled up in bed
  on cold winter nights
Covers pulled over my head
  and with a night light ballpoint pen
  and poetry journal in hand,
Scribbling down sweet phrases
  of love and longing
  stoking the fires of poesy
  enjoying the beauties of verse.
These are true joys of the poet's life.

"Mamu," ink on paper, Phyllis Parun, 1972.

THE POET'S CAT

Sleeping 'til dawn
The poet's cat
Has no visible means of support
Her only work remains
   the cleaning of her claws
   and the eating of uncountable nibbles
   then begging for more
   mostly for attention   rather than from hunger.

She is the well-fed pet of the poet
   lying around all day at the foot
   of the immobile writer
Who leaves her chair only to change chairs
While the only sound the cat hears
   is the scratching of the pen on paper
   or the spoon clank on the food bowl.

The poet's cat runs up and down the house
   her paws pounding noisily
   on the wooden floors
then sitting patiently on the
   rug designated for brushing her
   she waits for the scratching of the pen to stop
sometimes amusing herself with
any piece of string she can find.

The poet's cat is kind
The poet's cat is vigilant
   patiently waiting every morning
   for the Sun to rise
   for the candles to go out
   for the poet to tire
of the company of words
and be amused by her.

DOORS

Unafraid, they leave their doors   unlocked
these artists who live in wooden houses
   filled with books and paper,
   pens and paintbrushes.
What do these mean to a thief
   these tools of the creative,
   these materials that give form to ideas?
they cannot be resold
their value is not monetary -
Nothing   there can be stolen.

Unlocked and unafraid
   their doors open
   their souls unarmored
   vulnerable to the world
the creative ones leave traces
of where they have been.

EARLY MORNING

Early Morning in my antique house
built by immigrants, freemen and slaves
lived in by many cultures
commissioned by a Spanish man
with wife from Barcelona.
This house has many stories to tell.

Awakening to sounds of birds
watching the day's light slowly arrive
illuminating all the objects
in these rooms

The smell of shiitakes soaking
rice cooking, and soup simmering
completely fills my kitchen.

"Ghost Town," watercolor. Phyllis Parun, 2009.

GHOSTS

Ghostly figures
towering hauntingly
over tops of tombs
overcast by
ominous, stormy skies.
You know you're in New Orleans.

*"**My Room**,"* Carrollton Avenue, Phyllis Parun, 1967.

THE POET'S HOUSE

The poet's house is not cluttered
With meaningless trinkets
Purchased at a five-and-dime.
The poet does not surround herself
With culturally barren objects
Devoid of meaning.

In the poet's house every object
Holds a cherished memory
Of a dear friend or a gesture of good wishes
Or fond hellos.

The poet's house
Cradles books, poetry and art.
The poet explores life from inside out,
Turning down unknown paths
Going where others do not
Crafting sweet phrases
Holding up the mystery for all to see.

Spirit personified,
The poet is the best part of being human.

NO DOWN SPOUTS HERE

It rained today   and I
Sat in my garden
Sipping freshly steeped tea
Listening to the rain
Fall upon leaves.

Such peaceful stillness
In the cool breeze
With fresh air
Wet earth
Rustling leaves
Rainwater dripping from the gutters.
No down spouts here.

My cat dashing between drizzles
On her tippie toes
With such delicacy
That even the Queen would envy!

I lift the teacup to my lips
And toast Sayonara
To a departing dear friend.

LIONS

two sprawled there
yellow
two
on the
tomb stone white
both of them rest
at the entrance
guarding
the
place
called
Pritchard.

"Misfit," ink drawing, Phyllis Parun, 1983.

MISFIT

I fit nowhere
But misfit everywhere.
How about you,
Are you a misfit too?
Exclusive to none
Part of all -
Do you misfit
With the best of them too?

"Swans," photograph ,Phyllis Parun, 2017.

BITTERSWEET

Bittersweet are life's sorrows.
My dear Aunts, Father, Mother
And Brother
now all gone
and I, feeling a little like an orphan
look to my original family
the sun,
the moon,
the trees
and mother earth
to nurture me.

WORDS

One day I will die
Where will these words go then,
I wonder.
Is there a heaven for the best of them
Or maybe a purgatory for the naughty ones
that will not obey?
And, of course, there must be a Hell
where the worst of the bunch go
to live in the intolerable heat for all eternity.
And if they should ever repent their ways
can these then return to the land of the poets
to be crafted anew
and fashioned finally into
some extraordinary beauty?
I wonder.

"Self-Portrait," Phyllis Parun, 1956

BIO

ARTIST-PHILOSOPHER-POET
NATIVE TO NEW ORLEANS
SEVEN DECADES OF TECHNO-SOCIAL CHANGES
FROM ICE BOXES, WOOD BURNING STOVES
AND RADIOS, NO AC IN HOUSES OR AUTOS
(YES, VIRGINIA, THERE WAS SUCH A TIME!)
FROM RIDING THE CITY BUS TO SCHOOL
WITH A SIGN STARING ME IN THE FACE
WHICH READ "WHITES ONLY"
THRU NASA AND SPUTNIK
BEATNIKS, BEATLES, HIPPIES, YUPPIES,
POT, ACID, COKE, HEROIN.
FROM DOO-OP, ROCK 'N ROLL,
PROGRESSIVE JAZZ.
BLACK, WOMEN, GAY CIVIL LIBERITES
AND MARXISTS POLITICS,
PUNCH CARDS TO SMART PHONES -
PARADES, PARADES, PARADES,
MULTI CULTURES AND ETHNIC TRIBES
COMING AND GOING
NOT TALKING OF MICHELANGELO.
SO MANY YEARS OF ENTANGLEMENTS.
BORN A LUTHERAN NOW A TAOIST
IT'S HALF A CENTURY LATER.

Oh, beautiful moment
Precious illusion
Do not flee!

ACKNOWLEDGEMENTS

No one creates in a vacuum and I am most fortunate to be immersed in the caldron of raw inspiration and sheer synergy of my New Orleans community of creative people.

Special thanks to Karen E. Doby (Dancing Shark Studio) for editing and technical support with photographs and cover design. To Carolyn Wilenski Levy, Lee Meitzen Grue, Joe Clark, Bobbie Geary, Dr. Sandra Karp, Gloria Daniel, John B. Lafata for personal comments and for their many years of creative and inspirational friendships.

Part One

_____THE POEMS

"Life Leaves, " 2003.
;New Orleans, My Home," 2002.
"Childhood," Apr. 29, 2016.
"Flames," 1998.
"Early Memories," 2016.
"Gone," 1969.
"My Brother, Myself," 2015.
"Late Summer," 1998
"My Father, My Coach," 2017.
"Mementoes,"2015.
"Grandmother's House," 2016.
"The Singer," 2015.
"Retired," 2017.
"Rooting Around," 2015.
"Mother Music," 2017.
"Map," 2015.
"Tea Brews," 2003.

_____*ILLUSTRATIONS BY PHYLLIS PARUN*

"Lafitte's Blacksmith Shop," charcoal, 1956.
"The Family Room," 407 East Morris, Hammond, La., 1947.
"Backyard Dollhouse," Hammond, La., 1947.
"Sister, Brother," Studio Photographer, 1945.
"My Father, the gentleman sportsman," 2017.
"Archives," photograph, PhyllisParun, 2017.
"Grandmother Mana Parun and Family," photograph, 2017.
"Christabel," charcoal drawing, 1959.
"The Fibonacci Staircase," (Arne Jacobsen, Royal Hotel Copenhagen) photograph, 2003.
"My Mother, My Teacher," photograph, 2017.
"Self-Portrait," New Orleans, 2017.

Part Two

_____THE POEMS

"Sunrise Falls," 1998.
"Pilgrimage to Paris," 2000.
"The Line," 2011.
"That's a Nice Tomb," 2000.
"The Dancer," 2011.
"Immortality," 2017.
"Sunday," 2018
"Worship." 2018.
"Where Do I Live?" 1995.
"Aprés Déluge," 2011.
"Empty." 2003.
"Sunrise in Bywater," 1998.
"Doing Nothing, " for Taoist Teacher, Ken Cohen, 1998.
"Goddess," for Dr. Peter Kingsley, Esalen, 2004.
"Today," after Katrina, 2005.
"Ancient Oak," after Katrina, 2005.*

_____ *ILLUSTRATION BY PHYLLIS PARUN*

"Street in Paris," photograph, 2001.
"Line," ink on paper, 2016.
"St. Louis Cemetery #3(New Orleans), photograph, 1998.
"Dancer," ink on paper, 1984.
"Passage," (Copenhagen), photograph, 2002.
"Stravinsky's The Flood," glass window design, 1977.
"Moonscape ," ink on paper, 1996.
"Pilgrimage, " ink on paper, Phyllis Parun, 2002.
"Flood Water," gouache cut paper, 2012.
"Ancient Oak," ink on paper, 2002.

* (In 2005 after the Katrina flood, a 200 year old mighty oak by the bandstand had had its limbs brutally and senseless cut off by disaster chasers. Later we learned that City Park had lost 1000 oaks to disaster chasers earning $100 a tree.)

Part Three

_____THE POEMS

"Poetry Awaits," 2003.
"Beauty Salon," 2003.
"Artist's Model," 1994.
"Full of Youth," 2000.
"Age Approaches," 2003.
"Poet's Life," 2000.
"The Poet's Cat," 2017.
"Doors," 2016.
"Early Morning," 2001.
"Ghosts," 1996.
"The Poet's House," 2015.
"No Down Spouts," for Takako Kawano, 2000.
"Lions," 1969.
"Misfit," 2015.
"Life's Sorrows," 1998.
"Words," 2016.
"Bio," 2000.
"Beautiful Moment," 2018.

ILLUSTRATIONS BY PHYLLIS PARUN

"Artist's Model," ink on paper, 1994.
"Poet's Hours," ink on paper, 1983.
"Mamu," ink on paper, 1972.
"Ghost Town," watercolor, collaboration with
Australian watercolorist Moonyeen McNeilage, 2009.
"My Room," Carrollton Avenue, 1967.
"Misfit," ink drawing, 1983.
"Self-Portrait," pencil on paper, 1956
"Swans," photograph, 2017.

PHYLLIS PARUN

*N*ew Orleans native artist-philosopher-poet, pursued academics first at LSU New Orleans majoring in traditional western philosophy then at the University of Pennsylvania and LSU Baton Rouge, followed by a study of social sciences at Harvard with business and marketing at Delgado College.

*M*s. Parun has spent a large part of her adult life asking deep philosophical questions, creating art, writing, and doing cultural community work by founding several arts organizations, opening a Fine and Decorative Arts Studio restoring antique furniture and reviving three lost gilded arts: medieval gold leaf panel painting, etched glass gilding (Fr. *verre églomisé*) and gilded tooled metal bas relief.

*A*s an arts, health and social-political activist, Ms. Parun has been a catalyst shaping the unwritten culture of the New Orleans landscape.

*M*s. Parun has led a health conscious, artistic and literary life, devoting her time to exhibiting visual art of painting, drawing, sculpture, photography and publishing interviews, articles, essays, poems, e-zines, and short stories in a wide variety of national and local venues. While her health and happiness studies led her to learn barefoot shiatsu, macrobiotic cooking, Asian food energetics, plant-based nutrition and many forms of movement, exercise and sports including dance, yoga, qigong, indoor and outdoor team games from prominent figures in these respective fields.

*H*er writing is filled with her many rich and fulfilling life experiences. Ms. Parun is clearly one of New Orleans' native living treasures.

Published genres *includes: interviews, articles, essays, poems, e-zines, art, and photography in a wide variety of publications: The Beachcomber (LSUNO), Alternatives, Contemporary Arts Southeast, Macrobiotics Today, NonCredo, The Rogue, Pulse (AOBTA), American Assn. of Oriental Medicine, MacroNetjournal, Healthways, Bywater Current, Gulf Coast Arts Review, ArtLit, Iris, Qi: Journal of Traditional Eastern Health and Fitness, The New Laurel Review (2001, 2015), The Maple Leaf Rag III (2006), Mending for Memory (2017) and creator of The New Orleans Living Treasurers Award and The New Orleans Avant-Garde ezine*

End Notes

If you enjoyed this please leave a review at Amazon USA
https://www.amazon.com/-/e/B006HX9348

And visit artist-author webpage
https://www.phyllisparun.com

For future notifications on new releases,
join author email list:
pbpstudio@yahoo.com

F i N

www.ingramcontent.com/pod-product-compliance
Lightning Source LLC
Chambersburg PA
CBHW071215070526
44584CB00019B/3042